P9-DMI-754

42 MILES

Best Friends

Tamika dreams
of living in Milan,
designing the latest fashions
or modeling them in the pages
of *Vogue*.
She likes the four styles of dance
her mom insists she learn,
and she holds herself
so elegantly, as if a spotlight
follows her every move.
Only Annie and I
see her silly side:
the impersonations she does
of our teachers and parents
and the way she snorts
when she's laughing.

Annie's afraid
of everything:
Lyme disease
the speed of the bus
the additives in cafeteria food.
She wears her worry
in chewed fingernails
and eyes that flit around,
searching out danger.

So I got half of Dad's name:
Joseph
and part of Mom's, too:
Eleanor.
But no one calls me
by my real name:
JoEllen.

Mom (and my city friends)
call me Ellen,
and to Dad (and his family)
I've always been Joey.

Now my days—
divided between them—
are as different as my names.

Bargains

I look just like Mom—
hazel eyes
straight brown hair.
Even my dimples
match hers.
But I'm long and lean
like Dad,
the fifth-generation Courtney kid
to weave around the apple orchard
on this rolling Ohio farm.

The story goes
that Mom and Dad couldn't agree
on a name
(and a lot else, I guess,
since they divorced when
I was in diapers).

Changes

Until this year
my parents lived
four blocks apart
in Cincinnati.

Until this year
I went
to Liberty Elementary.

Until this year
I was average height
had clear skin
and didn't need glasses
to see the blackboard.

Everything
was easier
until this year.

MIX-AND-MATCH FACES

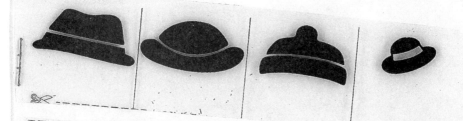

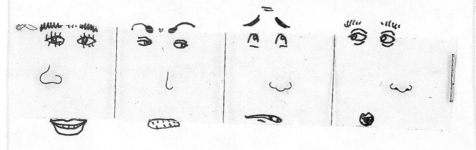

FOR TRISH DELONG—

498.98 MILES TOO FAR AWAY

—T. V. Z.

FOR JANEY, JULIE, AND DEANNE

—E. C.

*With thanks to Marcia Leonard for a journey of faith
and editing much longer than 42 miles—T.V.Z.*

Clarion Books
a Houghton Mifflin Company imprint
215 Park Avenue South, New York, NY 10003
Text copyright © 2008 by Tracie Vaughn Zimmer
Illustrations copyright © 2008 by Elaine Clayton

Cover Map © by Rand McNally, R.L. 07-S-121

The illustrations were executed in mixed media.
The text was set in 14-point Pastonchi.

www.clarionbooks.com

Printed in the U.S.A.

Library of Congress Cataloging-in-Publication Data
Zimmer, Tracie Vaughn.
42 miles / by Tracie Vaughn Zimmer ; [illustrations by Elaine
Clayton].
p. cm.
Summary: As her thirteenth birthday approaches, JoEllen decides to
bring together her two separate lives—one as Joey, who enjoys weekends
with her father and other relatives on a farm, and another as Ellen,
who lives with her mother in a Cincinnati apartment near her school
and friends.
ISBN 978-0-618-61867-5
[1. Divorce—Fiction. 2. Family life—Ohio—Fiction. 3. Schools—
Fiction. 4. Self-realization—Fiction. 5. Cincinnati (Ohio)—Fiction.
6. Ohio—Fiction. 7. Novels in verse.] I. Clayton, Elaine, ill. II. Title.
III. Title: Forty-two miles.

PZ7.5.Z63Aag 2008
[Fic]—dc22
2007031032

WOZ 10 9 8 7 6 5 4 3

Purchase Order: 4500225466

4
2

by **Tracie Vaughn Zimmer**

M
I
L
E
S

illustrated by **Elaine Clayton**

Clarion Books ◆ New York

Enough

Belinda James
cuts in line
in the lunchroom and at the fountain
sits on her throne
(a sink in the girls' room),
making snarky remarks that echo
around the pink-tiled walls.

Each week
she writes the Names of the Lame
("Ellen" has appeared twice so far)
on a mirror
in plum lipstick
she swears she stole from the drugstore.

She gets money
from people
who don't owe her,
and she rules the locker room
and the lunch tables, too.

Someday
someday soon
I'll have had enough of that,
Belinda James.

But she can take down
a two-hundred-pound man
in judo class
and wants to open her own dojo someday.

Me, I've tried
drama lessons (too embarrassing)
basketball (too exhausting)
ballet (too exacting).
And I went through three instruments
(flute, French horn, clarinet)
before I settled
on the saxophone.
I have no idea
where I want to live
or what kind of job
I might like to have.
But I'll try most anything
once.

Symmetry

In math class today
Mr. Howard showed us how
the line of symmetry
can divide a shape
precisely in half:
a hexagon
a butterfly
a sunflower's face,
the same on each side.

The formula for my life:
school days in the city with Mom
weekends on the farm with Dad
holidays, birthday, summer vacation—
all negotiated.

They try to split me
like an apple's pale heart
on either side of the blade,
pretending
my life is like
Mr. Howard's hexagon,
equal parts
no matter
how many times they cut it.

Friday Nights

Mom hovers in the doorway
as I stuff my backpack
with homework and music.
Don't need clothes;
there are plenty of worn ones
tucked in the painted dresser
under the attic eaves
at Dad's house.

No sleeping over with Annie and Tamika.
("Try to have fun in Hicktown," they say.)
No long Saturday afternoons spent
planning outfits
comparing quizzes in teen magazines
painting each other's nails
the same shade of glittery green.

On the drive to the farm
quiet falls like the darkness
the closer we get to Dad.

Soon I'll climb out of Mom's
crumbless black sedan,
and she'll call from the cracked-open window,
"See you Sunday, Ellen."

I'll walk in the house without knocking,
and Dad will be standing over the sink,
eating one of his odd concoctions—
meatball tacos or eggplant pizza.
"I tried to wait for ya, Joey,"
he'll say between bites.
Then he'll hand me a plate,
and my other life will begin.

Traveling Exhibit

A year after Papa died
Gran packed a U-Haul
(and her widowhood, she said)
and took off with her best friend
for Florida.
My dad settled into the farmhouse
and joined his brother, my Uncle Tilman,
in business,
converting the old barn
into an engine repair shop,
where they work together
every day.

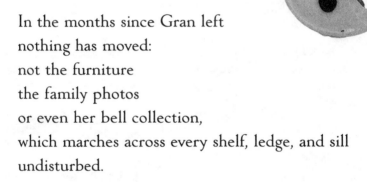

In the months since Gran left
nothing has moved:
not the furniture
the family photos
or even her bell collection,
which marches across every shelf, ledge, and sill
undisturbed.

Papa's tools still hang
in their assigned spaces
(a shadow beneath each one
on the faded pegboard).
The honeysuckle scent of Gran's perfume
hides behind closet doors.

The only change:
Dad sleeps in the large bedroom
that used to belong to his parents,
and I've inherited his old room—
drab, dingy, and decorated
with baseball trophies
and faded, dusty pennants.

I wonder if Dad will make this home his own,
or if I'll just be a traveling exhibit
in the museum
of the boy he used to be.

Hayden

My cousin Hayden
lives with his parents,
my Uncle Tilman and Aunt Shirley,
and two collies,
Rebel and Kate,
on the other side
of the apple orchard
in a double-wide trailer.

Hayden and I spend weekends
exploring the woods
trail riding
on Old Bess and Brownie
or catching sunfish with worms from the garden.
("Can't do *this* in the city," he says.)

Sometimes,
as we head down to the pond
in the last few minutes of slanting light,
Hayden grabs Papa's old five-string
or plucks a harmonica
from his pocket
to harmonize with the tunes of twilight.
The lightning bugs begin
to waltz in the darkening woods,
and we stay
until the stars slice holes
in the night.

Russell

Hayden had
an older brother—
Russell.
Tall
athletic
always quick with a joke.
Got killed by a drunk driver
the summer he turned sixteen.

Aunt Shirley
stopped babysitting
the preschoolers
who'd always filled her days
and her arms.

Uncle Tilman
sold his semi
and gave up his long-haul
truck routes
to tinker with engines,
stay closer to home.

And Hayden
started writing songs
that send his rich voice soaring,
like a kite trying to break free
from the hands of the wind.

42 Miles

After an early Sunday supper,
as daylight melts
into darkness,
Dad drives me
back to the city.

It takes nearly an hour to get
from the blue door
decorated with Gran's grapevine wreath
to the steel gray one
marked by iron numbers
and a peephole.

Penned in the small cage
of his faded red pickup,
Dad shares more words with me
than he does in
the rest of our hours together
combined.

With every mile the landscape changes—
trees and fields
morph into tall city buildings,
winding country road
into six-lane highway—

and Joey
transforms into
Ellen,
though no one notices
but me.

Mondays

If I were a teacher . . .

I wouldn't stand behind a table
or lecture at my wooden desk.
And I would never
talk behind my hand
to another teacher.

I'd let all the kids who did their best
on the thirty-word vocabulary test
(even if that was a C)
pull a homework pass or
have ten minutes longer for lunch.

Books would be sprinkled over every spare space—
even hung from the ceiling on string—
and I'd pluck one
to read aloud at odd times all day.
Homework would be optional.
Report cards wouldn't exist—
not to mention in-school suspension
or after-school detention for talking.

When spring finally packed away her winter coat,
I'd hold every class under the ancient elm,
who could finally hear the lessons
he'd only spied on before
from his seat outside the dirty windows.

The News

In a basket
next to a microwave
that's used only to pop popcorn,
Mom keeps a take-out menu
from every restaurant
in a ten-block radius.

She has a favorite at each one:
fried dumplings from Jo Jo's China Bistro
cheese enchiladas from El Loro
five-way chili from Skyline.
But I try something new
each time we order.

Even if I learn
that curry nauseates me
and that minestrone
is really just vegetable soup,
at least my tongue's not bored.

We eat
slumped over TV trays,
spilling details from our days
and rating the sizzling
fashions and trends
from the *Hollywood Tonight* show
that, when I was little,
I called "the news."

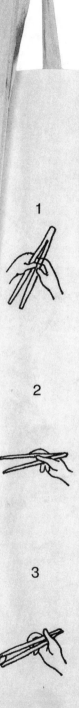

A Cut Above

Tuesdays after school
I meet Mom at
A Cut Above,
the salon where she styles hair.
While I do my homework
at the front desk,
I watch women
of all ages and sizes
sit in my mother's chair.

Some dig crumpled magazine pictures
out of purses,
point to famous movie stars
with perfect looks.
A few shrug their shoulders
when asked what they want,
trusting her cool fingers
to slenderize an apple face
or hide protruding ears.

Mom knows all their successes
and sorrows
but never gossips the way some people do.
She spirits their secrets
to the top shelf of her heart,
where she hides her own—
even from me.

Aunt Mimi's Attic

Mrs. Queen
(Tamika's mom)
owns Aunt Mimi's Attic,
the second-hand store
down on 29th and Orchard.
People bring her stuff
from attics and estate sales,
flea markets and basements:
claw-footed dressers
tin-can collections
war posters
dolls with missing eyes
moldy books
clothes that belong
in black-and-white films.

A single path weaves
through the jungle of junk.
Don't be tempted
to tug anything out.
Oh, no! That's liable to cause
an avalanche.
Ask Mrs. Queen;
she'll liberate what you want—
even offer ten percent off
if it's a gift
for somebody else.

After school
Tamika, Annie, and I
help her unload boxes
price things with round orange stickers
and sort them into their sections.
Mrs. Queen plays
vintage vinyl
while we work,
and we learn the lyrics
to songs
our grandmas once danced to,
though we can't picture them
ever being that young.

Rules

Homework before TV.

No R-rated movies.

Lights out by ten.

No pets allowed in.

Fresh fruit for snack.

Don't ever talk back.

With Mom,
it's all about
rules.

Just This Side of Chaos

When Dad lived in the city,
his place was always
piled with newspapers
magazines
and books—with unopened bills
as bookmarks.

I can tell
he's trying to be neater,
living in his parents' house.
(Can he hear Gran nagging
in his head?)

But he'll let me sleep
wherever I drop:
on the couch
on the porch
or even in the hayloft.
I've never had a bedtime
or curfew.
I can watch
whatever the TV will tune into,
read any book on the shelf.

We might eat
at six standing by the sink
or at ten sitting at the table.
With Dad, one thing's for certain:
nothing ever is.

Bookmobile

Each Saturday
when Dad closes up shop
in the old barn,
he calls for me as if dinner is served:
"Joey, bookmobile!"
Then we hike the half-mile trail
to His Holiness Abounds
Pentecostal Church, where the
library on wheels parks.
We pretend we're modern pioneers
in search of provisions—
and we are.
Dad owns only a tiny TV.
There's no cable service
or DVD player,
and the VCR's been broken
forever.

After we return home,
Dad and I invent
a new recipe using
ingredients from the garden
or from jars stored on the dusty shelves
in the basement.

We evaluate our creation.
Then we stretch out on the couch—
our feet sharing the ugly afghan
in the middle.
Matching lamps
glow over our heads,
and we disappear into dreams
of different worlds.

BOOK MOBILE

THE BOOK MOBILE

Please bring your boo
back to the Book Mobile
one week after you check
it out.

Inheritance

When asthma rips
my sleep wide open,
and my chest's angry demand
for a breath of cool air
leaves me gasping,
my dad
whispers, "I'm here, Joey. I'm here."
He folds himself beside my bed
while the medicine takes hold.
His calloused hands smooth back
the blanket of my hair,
and he hums hymns
he learned
when he was young
and his dad
did the same
for him.

Tractor

They say
a dog
is man's best friend,
but for my dad
it's always been
a tractor.
("Nothin' against dogs,
mind you . . .")
Because no matter how faithfully
a dog trots behind you
in a circle of never-ending chores,
it can't make you
feel like a king
riding over your own acres
at the end of the day,
the lavender light slanting
across your family's fields
and common dirt brushed like gold.

Opening Day

Opening day
of the Cincinnati Reds' baseball season
is Mom's self-proclaimed
holiday.

From our seats in the outfield
the players look like
toys,
but it's the people
in the stands
I watch anyway:

The beer vendor
who belts out like an opera tenor,
"Ice-cold beer hee-yah!"

A group of college guys
wearing tank tops
(though it's only fifty degrees)
showing off muscles
and newly minted tattoos
as they lean forward,
elbows on knees,
to exchange insults.

A row of five kids
in matching jerseys,
who suck the salt
from their peanuts
eat cotton candy and ice cream
ignore the game
until the seventh-inning stretch,
when they climb onto their seats
to sing every word of
"Take Me Out to the Ballgame."

Unlike me, Mom ignores everything
but the game,
tracks each play
in a secret code for serious fans,
as if she'll be reporting
from the dugout
for the sports channel
right after the game.

But if the bases are loaded
and the score tied,
I'll pitch my shyness
under the seat
stand tall as I can
and hoot and cheer
as though it's my own dad
up at home plate.

Dress Up

The back room of Aunt Mimi's Attic
is heaped with vintage clothes and costumes.
Tamika, Annie, and I
crack open
a pioneer's trunk
stuffed with fancy hats,
some as small and brittle as stale biscuits
others larger than pillowcases
and just as floppy!

We try everything on:
elbow-length gloves
with dainty pearl buttons
and delicate moth holes.
Stained corsets
with laces and straps.
Heavy, musty dresses
in fabrics that Tamika names:
gabardine, velvet, brushed-back satin,
calico, homespun.

The coats with fur collars
the feather boas
the clunky costume jewelry
all get us giggling—
don't ask me why.

Or maybe it's the crazy stage names
we call each other:
Xanadu
ZeZe and
Zephora.

Mrs. Queen hammers
the temperamental cash register twice
to open the drawer
hands us a few bills
to buy day-old doughnuts
from the bakery four doors down
and tells us
to get on out of her hair.

We change into our faded jeans
and sweatshirts
turn back into Tamika, Annie, and Ellen
and tumble out of the store,
arms draped around each other.

Whatever we wear
our friendship
fits.

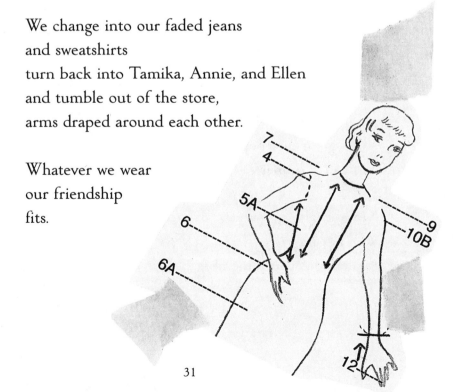

Movie Night

On Thursdays at six
Mom and I meet under the
antique marquee of the Commodore Theater.
The lobby is full of
faded, mismatched furniture.
There's a place in the carpet
that's so worn
it looks like a scraped knee.
And the gold tassels at the bottom
of the red velvet curtains
seem to unravel a bit more each week.
But I like this tattered elegance.

We watch
old black-and-white classics
subtitled art flicks
and third-run features.
We share
a large tub of popcorn
a bag of red licorice
and a giant diet pop
and call it dinner.

Mom might annoy me
with her nagging
("Ellen, did you remember . . ."),

but there's always this
Thursday night truce
waiting for us
in front of the flickering screen.

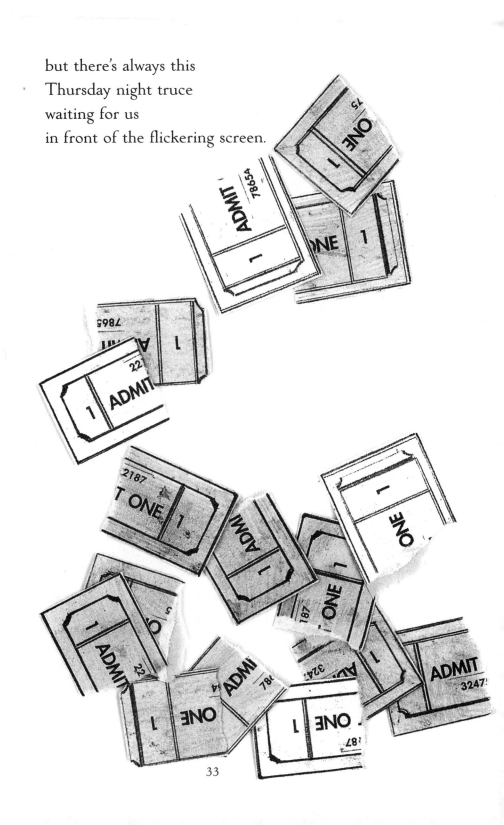

I Love

I love . . .

The smell of a Macintosh apple
just overripe.
My new kitten heels
ticking down city streets.
Bubble baths so hot
they turn my skin pink.
Scrambled eggs
with melted American cheese.
Listening to bluegrass
and playing saxophone.
The weight of my backpack
after a bookmobile visit.
Mom's fingers
braiding my hair.
Dad's voice
soothing the farm animals.
Tamika's opinions
Annie's giggle
Hayden's songs . . .

and making lists
like this one.

B*l*ues

Outside the shoe store
on a three-legged stool
a scruffy man
in a ratty coat
plays a saxophone
that looks as if it's been used
for batting practice.

In front of him
the instrument case
is left open
like a hungry mouth,
the red velvet lining
peeling from each corner.

People sometimes pitch in
coins from their pockets
but rarely even turn
their heads
or stop
to listen
to the mournful sound
his horn makes.

I do.

Hands

Old Mr. Johnson owns the farm
just up a piece.
He rents out all his acres
save three
where he plants a garden
each spring,
churning the rich soil
with his old hand plow,
spending long days out
in its rippled rows,
the corn slowly swallowing
his crumpled frame
as the summer winds on.

His sons grew up
and left the farm,
putting their faith in factories
instead of the weather.
"Smarter 'n me, I s'pect,"
he says,
sipping bitter black coffee
on his creaky porch swing,
waving at each passing car,
hoping somebody
(like Dad and me)
will stop and sit for a spell

to compare this year's harvest
to last
and all the others
his hands have known.

Missing

Ever since Hayden and I
were little,
when the apple trees put on
their white veils in April
and tossed handfuls of confetti
in celebration of spring,
Gran
would bake
oatmeal-raisin cookies,
and Papa would crank out
cinnamon ice cream,
in the same wooden bucket
he'd used as a kid.

Hayden and I would make
cardboard crowns
with pennies glued on as jewels,
and Gran would declare us
King and Queen of Spring.

Hayden and I made a batch
of cinnamon ice cream on Saturday;
but it tasted
like something lost.

Farm Nights

The apple trees
share secrets.

The ducks endlessly discuss
the quality of rain.

A freight train
moans its lonely call.

Whoever thinks
it's quiet in the country
has never slept here
before.

Cincinnati Nights

Through my open window:
the streetlight,
my nightlight.

An ambulance wailing
cars cussing
cats calling
dogs delivering the news.

My city
lullaby.

Fine

Each week
Mom and Dad ask
ever so politely
about each other.
I've learned over the years
that the only answer they really want to hear
is a mumbled "Fine. Just fine."

I never tell Mom
how I love to cook
with Dad—
inventing new dishes,
tossing ingredients
into the sizzling olive oil—
then discussing our creations
as we devour them.

And I never describe for Dad
Mom's modern apartment—
her splashy use of color
and funky fabrics,
how we're always rearranging rooms,
then evaluating our designs.

Mom doesn't see Joey.
Dad rarely meets Ellen.
And no one ever asked
if that's fine, just fine
with me.

A u *t o* b i o g r a p h y

Ms. Oravec—
Language Arts, fourth period
and my favorite teacher by far—
has just assigned
an autobiography project:
the story of our childhood
a personal epiphany
an influential person
and an interview.

But I don't know
which life to describe,
Joey's or Ellen's,
and it's not as if Mom and Dad
share stories of my childhood
over the birthday candles each spring
or even
inhale the same air
if they can avoid it.

This assignment
makes running the seven-minute mile
in gym class
seem painless by comparison.

Regular

Every Wednesday at four
the bell jingles on the door
of Aunt Mimi's Attic.
Precious comes in first—
a yappy teacup poodle sporting a rhinestone collar—
followed by Mrs. Durango,
who holds the other end of the red leather leash.

Pick pick pick.
The pup paces the tile floor.
Pock pock pock.
Her owner's high heels answer.
Mrs. Durango turns china
upside down,
studying the maker's marks
with a magnifying glass
mined from her vintage designer bag.

She pays with cash from a neat roll of bills
she takes from a silk-embroidered change purse.
Then they go to the coffee shop next door,
where Mrs. Durango sips tea
slips bits of gourmet cookie
under the table to Precious
and writes letters on fancy stationery
to her husband,

who they say
never did come home
from the Vietnam War.

Toes

The girls' room is crowded
after lunch,
but even so,
Annie and Tamika wait for me
while I wash my hands.
Poised to write on the mirror
with her plum lipstick,
Belinda snips, "Hurry up, Ellen.
You don't want to keep
Tamika the Trash Queen
waiting."

(The room is suddenly
silent as stone.)

Tamika pulls her books
tight against her chest
bites her lip
so the tears won't spill
turns on her toe
like the dancer she is
and walks out,
never looking back.

Surprising everyone,
including myself,
I step hard
on Belinda's sandaled toes
put my dripping hands on her shoulders
and snap:
Don't Ever. Call her that. Again.

(Annie's mouth
hangs wide open—
wordless, for once.)

Empty Space

Annie and Tamika
never ask about my
life on the farm,
and I don't offer
particulars:
trail riding with Hayden
listening to bluegrass
slopping out stable muck
in ripped jeans and work boots.

Hayden doesn't know
about my city life:
listening to street music
wearing vintage fashions
working at the secondhand store
with Annie and Tamika.

All my unspoken words
create an empty space between us
where the truth hides.

Questions

Will I risk
a zero
against my string of straight As
just to avoid writing
my autobiography?

Will I gamble
that Ms. Oravec
won't call Mom
about the zero
since I'm one of her best
students?

Will I
disappoint
my favorite teacher

or
just
myself?

sin

The voice
of Papa's banjo comes
alive again in Dad's hands.
Hayden's fingers
follow the melody on his guitar.
And Aunt Shirley,
who speaks in whispers
and often to the floor,
sings as if in answer
to the geese
winging their way home
in spring.

The firelight
leaps on their faces.
The silver undersides
of the beech leaves
glow like dreams
above us.

Would it be a sin
to admit
that it's easier to believe the words
of the songs my aunt sings—

"I'll Fly Away"
"Amazing Grace"
"Down at the River"—
here under the cathedral of stars
than in the little white chapel
we go to
on Sunday mornings?

Proof

Searching for Gran's button collection
in a dark, dusty corner of the attic,
I find a box
marked *Joseph & Eleanor*
that holds the letters
notes
faded cards
and documents of my birth,
all the dates and details
I need to (finally) write my
autobiography.

Plus
a stack of pictures of my parents
holding hands or arm in arm:
at the roller rink (where they met)
the prom
their high school graduation
and their wedding (where they look
impossibly young).
And finally
grainy snapshots
of me displayed between them,
the glue
that failed to keep their marriage
together.

Holding the proof that they shared
love
and not just regrets,
I realize
they don't see in me
the mirror image of their mistakes—
or even what they hated in each other—
but the best that
each of them had to offer.

Thirteen

I turn thirteen
in three weeks' time.
But this year,
for a change,
I don't want
Mom and some Italian waiters
singing "Happy Birthday"
to me one night,
and Dad and his family
singing an encore days later.

No.
My two lives
are going to meet
and shake hands.
I'm going to have:
one celebration
one cake
and one song,
with all my favorite voices
singing together.

And when I make a wish
over my birthday candles,
I'm saying it out loud:

I want everyone to call me
by my whole, real name:
JoEllen,
'cause I'll be the one
to define myself,
thank you.

And this is just
the beginning.

The New Me

The old me
would've missed out
on everything.
The new me
called Dad
canceled my weekend
on the farm
and went to see
Tamika's dance recital
Annie's judo competition
and a jazz showcase downtown.

The new me asked Dad
if I could invite Annie and Tamika
out to the farm
at least once a month
and have a room
that's truly my own.

The new me
described the grand slam
that ended the Reds'
six-game losing streak.

Have you met the new me yet?

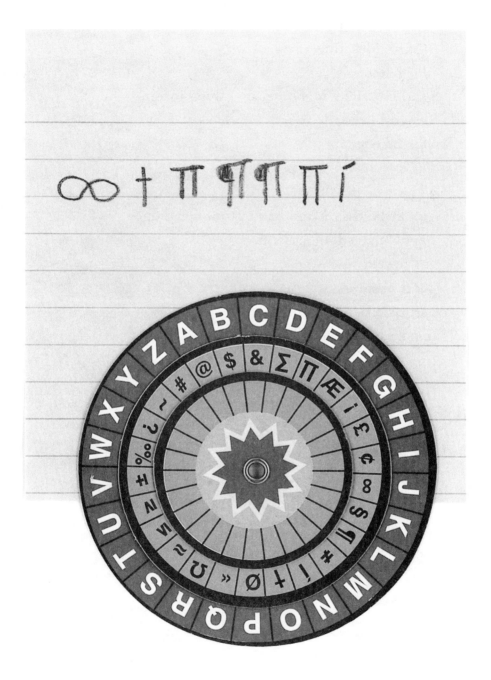

The New Me Again

The old me
would've ordered #3
(fried dumplings)
for Mom
and let Mr. Wu choose something for me
when I called Jo Jo's
for takeout.

The new me
took the cash Mom had left me for dinner
bought fresh ingredients
at the organic market
and made
sautéed peppers and chicken
and pasta with tomato basil sauce.

The old me
would've apologized
when Mom seemed taken aback
by my efforts
and wanted to know
who had taught me to cook.

The new me
described the best dishes
Dad and I have created
and told her
I'd like to cook twice a week
from now on.

I like this girl,
the new me.

While I'm at It

I tell Annie and Tamika
that I listen to bluegrass,
but I don't want to hear
the word "hick" from them,
ever again.

I convince Hayden that the city,
my city, Cincinnati,
holds more than concrete and crime,
and I'll show him its secrets
if he'll only
open his eyes.

I tell Mom
that I need a whole new look:
a sleek, chin-length bob.
She's teary at first
but finally agrees,
cutting off eleven inches
even highlighting what's left.
Then we bind my old ponytail
with rubber bands,
slip it into an envelope
to donate to kids who have cancer.

I choose new glasses
that make me
feel sophisticated
and at least
fifteen.

And when I'm done,
I barely recognize
the girl
smiling back at me
from the mirror.

Standing up for JoEllen

I'm in the lunch line
with Annie and Tamika,
talking over our weekend plans,
when Belinda tries to push
past me
the way she always does.
I block her way.
"Nice *hair*," she snorts,
obviously meaning the opposite.

(Conversations halt.
Everyone stares.)

"Yeah. I think so, too," I say sweetly.
"And the line, Belinda—
the line ends back there."

She turns and leaves,
going where?
No one cares.

And me, I feel taller
than I ever have,
and I collect all the
smiles
nods
and you-told-hers
and pocket them
like coins I have earned.

On the Same Block

It's the first weekend
for Annie and Tamika
out on the farm,
and tonight
I've planned
the best birthday ever:
a trip to the county fair.

But as much as I want
my cousin and my friends
to meet,
I keep imagining
a thick silence
hanging
like a curtain
between them.

And after we pile into
Aunt Shirley's van,
the first few minutes
do seem to spin
in slow motion.

But Annie's incessant chatter,
her curse at school,
turns out to be a magic potion
inside the crowded van.

The topics
tumble out:
favorite movies
books
classes
songs. . . .

And in no time
it feels as if
the four of us
grew up
on the same block.

County Fair

Who doesn't love a fair?
Foot-long hotdogs
cotton candy
caramel apples
and funnel cake dusted
with powdered sugar.
Rickety rides—
spinning, swirling, bumping—
and the view from the top
of the Ferris wheel,
where you can pretend
that everyone below
is as happy as you.

Fairy lights twinkle
around the awnings of the games.
Hayden wins a giant gorilla
by popping three balloons with a dart
carries it piggyback
the rest of the night
and then gives it to me
for my birthday.

My plan, a masterpiece—
even though Mom and Dad
just trade nods
and tight smiles

then go their separate ways
until we all meet
at the picnic shelter at eight,
to share the birthday cake
Dad baked and brought along.

Uncle Tilman shakes Mom's hand
as if he's meeting her for the first time.
But Aunt Shirley folds
her into her arms,
and the two of them hug
like the old friends
they used to be.

The four of us kids
(plus one gorilla)
stuff ourselves
into a photo booth.
And when the pictures
drop into the slot,
Tamika writes
(in her perfect lettering)
on the back
of each strip:
JoEllen's 1st birthday!

Presents

This weekend
Annie, Tamika, and I
will transform Dad's boyhood room
into my country kingdom.
We'll pack away his old stuff
paint the walls
(fuchsia or lavender, maybe)
hang curtains and posters
and frame a few of the photos
I found in the attic.
We'll stay up late
doing all the things
I usually miss.

Hayden promised
he'd round up Old Bess and Brownie
with the collies
and take Annie and Tamika
for a first-time ride.
And when sun sets on the lake,
he'll teach us to play a firefly waltz
on harmonicas that Mrs. Queen gave us.

Next weekend
Hayden will visit Cincinnati.
We'll all go see the Reds play Houston
and catch a movie at the Commodore,
and I'll play him my sax solo
from the spring band concert
he didn't get to hear.

Through it all
one part of me will be
with my cousin and my friends,
and another part
will be watching
as though it's a play
and I'm in the audience,
catching every word.

The Poems I Like Best

The poems I like best
wear classic black
with vintage accessories
and smell like a new book,
the spine just cracked.
They're the chitchat overheard on a city bus
or nonsense
volleyed between toddlers
on swings at the park.

My favorite poems
squeeze your hand
on a crowded street and say:
Look.

The poems I like best
wear blue jeans
and smell
like the tack room of a barn:
worn leather and horse.
They're the varied verses
of a mockingbird's song
or syllables traded between brothers
scratching scruffy chins
over the dark mysteries of an engine.

My favorite poems
hold a wooden spoon of words
and whisper:
Taste.

Someday

Someday, maybe,
I'll open my
own restaurant
on the tiptop of one of
Cincinnati's seven hills
or on the highest floor
of the tallest building
downtown.
My restaurant, JoEllen's,
won't have a menu.
I'll just invent a new dish
every night.

On weekends
I'll stay in a cottage
in the country,
with a collie dog
two Arabian horses
and no crops to tend.
And on Sundays
I'll crack open
a new book with breakfast
and won't close it
until dusk swirls her pastel skirts
around me.

Then I'll dance with her
barefoot
out on the damp lawn.